DELICIOUS

WHEAT-FREE
DAIRY-FREE

Oasis-Kitchen.com

Rita Mustafa, Holistic Nutritionist

ISBN: 978-0-9867558-0-4

Printed in Canada

The information presented in this book is based on the training, experience and research of the author. The suggestions in this book are not intended as a substitute for consulting with your health care provider.

Published by Art BookBindery

Photographs by Kim Hewitt

www.alyakphoto.com

How to Order:

Copies can be ordered online at www.Oasis-Kitchen.com or www.OasisHealth.ca

Or by calling 416-312-7617

Quantity discounts are also available for nutritionists, naturopathic doctors, bookstores and health food stores.

Visit us online at www.Oasis-Kitchen.com

Or visit our blog at
http://www.oasis-kitchen.com/blog

Contents

"Let thy food be thy medicine and thy medicine be thy food."

Hippocrates (460-377 B.C.)

Introduction

For as long as I can remember I have always been interested in health and nutrition. While I thought I was living a healthy lifestyle as a vegetarian, I suffered recurring sinus infections, digestive problems, fatigue and headaches. This eventually lead me to seek answers that did not involve popping pills. Today, as a Holistic Nutritionist, I have combined my knowledge, passion and experience to help others achieve optimal health through nutrition.

This cookbook is a collection of wheat-free and dairy-free recipes which I use in my home. They have been tried, tested and shared with many clients through the years.

Although wheat and dairy are not the only foods that have become known to affect people's health, this cookbook focuses on eliminating those particular foods.

In my practice, I see many clients with a variety of food intolerances, wheat and dairy being the most common. Undiagnosed food sensitivities are very common in our society and are often at the root of a many health conditions. A true food allergy is not the same as a food sensitivity (*or intolerance*).

Food sensitivities or intolerances can easily be identified by following an elimination diet or through blood testing done by your alternative health care practitioner.

The symbols opposite accompany each recipe, as appropriate, for easy identification. In addition, each recipe is featured in a full colour photo.

Whether you follow a wheat-free and dairy-free diet because of dietary restrictions, or because you choose to eat more healthful foods, I hope you enjoy the recipes provided.

WHEAT FREE

DAIRY FREE

GLUTEN FREE

VEGETARIAN

VEGAN

EGG FREE

SOY FREE

NUT FREE

Ingredients Used in this Cookbook

The ingredients used in this cookbook are readily available at your local health food stores and large chain supermarkets.

Agave Syrup
Derived from the agave cactus, native to Mexico. Raw honey or pure maple syrup can be substituted for most recipes.

Almond Butter
A butter made from ground almonds. Other nut and seed butters include cashew, sunflower, hazelnut and peanut butters.

Almond Milk
A dairy-free alternative. If allergic to nuts, rice milk can be substituted.

Apple Cider Vinegar
Unpasteurized, raw vinegar with many health benefits.

Bragg All Purpose Seasoning (Liquid Soy)
A liquid protein concentrate, derived from soybeans, which is unfermented and gluten free. Wheat-free soy sauce or tamari sauce can be substituted.
Note: Also known as Bragg Liquid Aminos

Brown Rice Flour
Flour which has been ground from unhulled rice kernels. Naturally gluten free. Can be found at most health food stores and bulk food stores.

Brown Rice Pasta
A wheat-free and gluten-free pasta made from brown rice. Other gluten-free pastas available on the market include corn and buckwheat pastas.

Ingendients Used in this Cookbook

Coconut Butter (*also known as coconut oil*)
Used as a healthy substitute for shortening and butter.
Note: Do not use extra virgin coconut butter unless recipe calls for it.

Coconut Flour
Finely ground coconut meat with most of the fat and moisture removed.

Coconut Milk
Made from the pressing of fresh, ripe coconut meat. A great substitute for milk or cream.
Note: Do not use "light" or "low-fat" coconut milk unless the recipe calls for it.

Cornstarch
Primarily used as a thickening agent. If allergic to corn, substitute with tapioca flour which is derived from the cassava plant.

Flax Oil (unrefined)
High in beneficial Omega-3 essential fatty acids (EFAs), which can help reduce inflammation in the body, relieve eczema, increase immune system function and balance hormone function.
Note: Not recommended for cooking.

Goji Berries
These high anti-oxidant berries can be found at your local health food stores and bulk food stores.

Hemp Seeds
An excellent source of the Omega-3 and Omega-6 essential fatty acids (EFAs), which can help reduce inflammation in the body, relieve eczema, increase immune system function and balance hormone function.

Ingredients Used in this Cookbook

Medjool dates
Medjool dates are large moist dates approximately 2½ times larger than regular cooking dates.

Miso
A fermented soybean paste originating from Japan. Miso ranges in color from white to brown. The lighter varieties are less salty and more mellow in flavour while the darker varieties have a more intense flavour.

Quinoa—pronounced 'keen-wa'
Provides a good source of vegetable protein. Technically not considered a grain but a seed. Quinoa seeds and quinoa flour are both wheat free and gluten free.

Rice Bran
An excellent gluten-free source of dietary fibre, used in place of wheat bran. Found at most health food stores. Oat bran can be substituted but is not considered gluten free.

Safflower Oil (unrefined)
Safflower oil is an excellent all-purpose oil.

Spelt Flour
Spelt is an ancient grain with a mellow, nutty flavour. Used as a substitute for wheat flour. Kamut flour can also be used as a substitute for wheat or spelt flours.
Note: "Light" spelt flour has had much of the germ and bran removed and is therefore not considered a whole-grain product.

Ingredients Used in this Cookbook

Sucanat Sugar

Sucanat (which stands for "Sugar Cane Natural") is sugar in its most natural form. Water is evaporated from the freshly squeezed juice of the sugar cane, leaving behind many vitamins and minerals, making it a healthful alternative to white, refined sugar.

Tahini (*also known as sesame butter or paste*)

Tahini is made from pureed sesame seeds and is a major ingredient in hummus and other dishes from the Middle East.

Tapioca Flour

Tapioca flour adds chewiness to baking and is a good thickener. Tapioca flour is derived from the cassava plant and is both wheat free and gluten free.

Vegetable Broth

Vegetables provide the body with alkaline properties. Make your own broth or choose organic store-bought varieties. If concerned about the salt content of store-bought broth use half the amount called for in a recipe and replace the rest with water.

Wakame—pronounced 'wah-kah-me'

Wakame is a type of seaweed or sea vegetable popular in Japan and is loved for its subtle flavour and slightly chewy texture. Other sea vegetables include kelp, dulse, arame and can be found at most health food stores.

Wheat-Free Bread Crumbs

Available at most health food stores but can easily be made at home. Use wheat-free or gluten-free crackers and process them in a blender or food processor until fine. Store in an airtight container.

Breakfast Foods

Quinoa Bran Muffins

Quinoa Bran Muffins

WHEAT FREE

DAIRY FREE

VEGETARIAN

SOY FREE

1 cup almond milk
2 tsp. apple cider vinegar
¼ cup quinoa flour
¾ cup spelt flour
¼ tsp. sea salt
1½ tsp. baking powder
½ tsp. baking soda
⅓ cup sucanat sugar
¼ cup safflower oil or melted coconut butter
⅛ cup organic molasses
2 eggs
1 cup rice bran
½ cup raisins
½ cup chopped walnuts

Preheat oven to 425°F.
Line a 12-cup muffin pan with paper baking cups.

In a measuring cup, combine almond milk and apple cider vinegar.
Stir and set aside for 5 minutes until curdled.

Sift quinoa flour, spelt flour, sea salt, baking powder and baking
soda into a small bowl and set aside.

In a large bowl, mix together sugar and oil with a hand mixer until
well combined. Add in molasses, eggs and almond milk mixture.
Mix again until well combined. Fold in rice bran, flour mixture,
raisins and walnuts just until blended. Do not over mix.

Spoon batter into prepared muffin cups.
Bake 18 to 20 minutes or until wooden toothpick inserted in the
center comes out clean.

 NUT FREE

- Replace almond milk with rice milk
- Omit walnuts

Makes 12 muffins

Zucchini Muffins

A gluten-free, moist and easy-to-make muffin.

WHEAT FREE

DAIRY FREE

GLUTEN FREE

VEGETARIAN

SOY FREE

1 cup brown rice flour
2 tsp. baking powder
½ tsp. baking soda
1 tsp. cinnamon
2 eggs
½ cup agave syrup
3 tbsp. safflower oil
1 tsp. vanilla extract
1 cup shredded carrots
1 cup shredded zucchini
½ cup chopped walnuts

Preheat oven to 375°F.
Line a 12-cup muffin pan with paper baking cups.

Sift the rice flour, baking powder, baking soda and cinnamon into a small bowl and set aside.

In a large bowl, whisk together the eggs, agave syrup, oil and vanilla. Stir in shredded carrots and zucchini.

Add sifted flour mixture to the zucchini mixture. Stir to incorporate all the flour. Fold in walnuts.

Spoon the batter into prepared muffin cups.
Bake 18 to 20 minutes or until wooden toothpick inserted in the center comes out clean.

 NUT FREE

- Omit walnuts

Makes 12 muffins

Zucchini Muffins

Cocoa Carrot Muffins

Cocoa Carrot Muffins

Fresh carrots and beets keep these muffins moist.

WHEAT FREE

DAIRY FREE

GLUTEN FREE

VEGETARIAN

SOY FREE

NUT FREE

1 cup brown rice flour
2 tsp. baking powder
½ tsp. baking soda
1 tsp. cinnamon
2 tbsp. cocoa powder
2 eggs
½ cup agave syrup
3 tbsp. safflower oil
1 tsp. vanilla extract
1 cup shredded carrots
1 cup shredded beets

Preheat oven to 375°F.
Line a 12-cup muffin pan with paper baking cups.

Sift the brown rice flour, baking powder, baking soda, cinnamon
and cocoa powder into a small bowl and set aside.

In a large bowl, whisk together the eggs, agave syrup, oil and vanilla.
Stir in shredded carrots and beets.

Gradually add the sifted flour mixture into the carrot mixture. Stir to
incorporate all the flour.

Spoon batter into prepared muffin cups.
Bake 18 to 20 minutes or until wooden toothpick inserted in the
center comes out clean.

Makes 12 muffins

Crêpes

*These gluten-free crêpes can even be used to make
delicious sandwich wraps, just omit the agave syrup!*

WHEAT FREE

DAIRY FREE

GLUTEN FREE

VEGETARIAN

SOY FREE

1 to 2 tsp. coconut butter or safflower oil, divided
½ cup brown rice flour
1 tsp. baking powder
⅛ tsp. sea salt
1 egg
1 tbsp. agave syrup
¾ cup to 1 cup almond milk

Heat a skillet or crêpe pan over medium-high heat. Add ¼ teaspoon
coconut butter or oil to the skillet and brush to coat the bottom of the
skillet (*repeat this step before making each crêpe*).

Mix the flour, baking powder and sea salt in a small bowl and set
aside.

In a large bowl, whisk together egg and agave syrup.   Sift in the
flour mixture and whisk until all the flour has been incorporated.

Slowly whisk in the milk until it forms a thin batter. Allow batter to
sit 10 to 15 minutes.

Pour a small amount (*about ¼ cup*) of batter into skillet. Tilt the pan
to spread batter into a thin, circular layer.

Cook the crêpe about 1 to 2 minutes, until you can slide a thin
spatula under the crêpe and gently flip it over. Cook about a minute
longer, just until golden. Transfer to a plate and cover.

Repeat with remaining batter, remembering to grease the skillet with
oil each time.

Serve with fresh fruit, pure maple syrup or agave syrup.

 NUT FREE   •   Replace almond milk with rice milk

Makes 6 crêpes

Pancakes with blueberry
agave syrup and fresh fruit
(page 17)

Crêpes with fresh fruit

Pancakes

Delicious gluten-free pancakes with a consistency and taste comparable to those made with wheat flour.

WHEAT FREE

DAIRY FREE

GLUTEN FREE

VEGETARIAN

SOY FREE

2 to 3 tbsp. coconut butter or safflower oil, divided
1 cup brown rice flour
2 tsp. baking powder
½ tsp. baking soda
2 eggs
2 tbsp. agave syrup
1 tsp. vanilla extract
1½ to 2 cups almond milk

Heat a large skillet or griddle over medium-high heat. Add enough coconut butter or cooking oil to coat the cooking surface.

In a small bowl, combine brown rice flour, baking powder and baking soda.

In a large bowl, whisk together eggs, agave syrup, 2 tablespoons coconut butter or oil and vanilla.

Sift flour mixture into egg mixture. Slowly whisk in enough milk to create a thick batter.

Pour a small amount (*about ¼ cup*) of batter into skillet. Cook until bubbles begin to form on the surface of the pancake. Flip and continue cooking until golden brown on bottom. Repeat with remaining batter.

Serve with fresh fruit, agave syrup or pure maple syrup.

 NUT FREE

- Replace almond milk with rice milk.

Makes 10 pancakes

Goji Berry Balls

*If you don't have cashew butter choose your
favourite nut or seed butter instead!*

¼ cup chopped, medjool dates
¼ cup goji berries
¼ cup cashew butter
⅛ cup agave syrup
¼ cup rice cereal
¼ cup finely chopped cashews

WHEAT FREE
DAIRY FREE
GLUTEN FREE
VEGETARIAN
VEGAN
SOY FREE
EGG FREE

In a small bowl, soak dates and goji berries in hot water for 5
minutes, just until softened. Drain and set aside.

In a food processor, add softened dates and goji berries, cashew
butter, agave syrup and cereal. Process for several seconds until well
combined. The mixture should hold its shape when formed into a
ball. (*If too dry, add 1 teaspoon of water at a time until it holds its
shape. If too wet and sticky, add more rice cereal and process until
no longer sticky.*)

Shape into walnut-sized balls and roll into chopped cashews.
Refrigerate until ready to serve.

NUT FREE

- Replace cashew
butter with
sunflower or
pumpkin seed butter
and the chopped
cashews with
chopped sunflower
or pumpkin seeds.

Makes 12 balls

Honey Nut Granola

Be creative and add a variety of nuts and seeds to suit your taste.

WHEAT FREE
DAIRY FREE
VEGETARIAN
EGG FREE
SOY FREE

4 cups organic rolled oats
1 cup nuts and seeds, chopped
(*almonds, walnuts, cashews, sunflower, pumpkin or sesame seeds*)
⅓ cup coconut butter
½ cup honey
1 tbsp. ground cinnamon
1 tsp. vanilla extract
1 cup mixed nuts, seeds and/or dried fruit, reserved

Preheat oven to 325°F.
Line a large shallow baking sheet with parchment paper.

In a large bowl, combine oats, chopped nuts and seeds and set aside.

Place coconut butter, honey and cinnamon in the top of a double boiler. Place over gently simmering water; upper pan should not touch water. Heat mixture until warm, but do not boil. Remove from heat and stir in vanilla.

Pour warm honey mixture over the oat mixture and stir until all ingredients are coated evenly.

Spread oat mixture onto prepared baking sheet.
Bake 20 to 25 minutes, stirring occasionally, until lightly browned.

Cool completely. Stir in reserved nuts, seeds and/or dried fruit. Store in an airtight container for up to 2 weeks.

Sprinkle over your favourite dairy-free ice cream or fresh fruit. Can also be eaten as a cereal with warm or cold dairy-free milk.

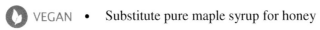 VEGAN • Substitute pure maple syrup for honey

Makes approx. 5 cups

Oatmeal Raisin Cookies

WHEAT FREE
DAIRY FREE
VEGETARIAN
VEGAN
SOY FREE
EGG FREE
NUT FREE

⅓ cup coconut butter
¼ cup agave syrup or sucanat sugar
2 tsp. organic molasses
1 tsp. vanilla extract
1 cup spelt flour
1 tsp. baking soda
1 tsp. cinnamon
1 cup oats
¼ cup raisins
¼ cup shredded or flaked coconut (*optional*)

Preheat oven to 350°F.
Line a small baking sheet with parchment paper.

In top part of double boiler, melt coconut butter over gently
simmering water; upper pan should not touch water.

Once melted, remove from heat and cool slightly (*about 2 minutes*)
before adding agave syrup, molasses and vanilla.

Sift in the spelt flour, baking soda and cinnamon followed by the
oats. With a fork, combine all ingredients.

Mix in the raisins and coconut (if using).

With your hands, shape into 8 balls and place on prepared baking
sheet. Flatten each cookie using the palm of your hand or a fork.

Bake 12 to 15 minutes or until edges are lightly browned.

Note: Cookies will still be soft when removed from oven but will
firm up once cooled.

Makes 8 cookies

Oatmeal Raisin Cookies

Banana Muffins

WHEAT FREE

DAIRY FREE

VEGETARIAN

SOY FREE

Muffins
3 ripe organic bananas
½ cup sucanat sugar
1 tbsp. safflower oil
1 tsp. vanilla extract
2 eggs
2 cups spelt flour
2 tsp. baking powder
½ tsp. baking soda
2 tsp. cinnamon
1 cup chopped walnuts

Topping (*optional*)
¼ cup finely chopped walnuts
1 tbsp. sucanat sugar

Preheat oven to 350°F.
Line a 12-cup muffin pan with paper baking cups.

In a large bowl, mash bananas. Add sugar, oil, vanilla and eggs. Mix with a hand mixer until well combined. Set aside.

Sift flour, baking powder, baking soda and cinnamon into a separate bowl.

Gradually add flour mixture into the banana mixture and mix until flour has been incorporated. Fold in walnuts.

Spoon batter into prepared muffin cups.
If desired, combine topping ingredients in a small bowl and sprinkle over unbaked muffins.

Bake 20 to 25 minutes or until a wooden toothpick inserted in center comes out clean.

 NUT FREE   •   Omit walnuts

Makes 12 muffins

Banana Muffins

Pumpkin Muffins

A moist and tasty gluten-free muffin.

Pictured on page 26 using a pumpkin-shaped muffin pan.

WHEAT FREE

DAIRY FREE

GLUTEN FREE

VEGETARIAN

SOY FREE

NUT FREE

Muffins
3 eggs
2 tbsp. coconut butter, melted
¼ cup pumpkin puree
⅓ cup sucanat sugar
½ tsp. cinnamon
¼ tsp. allspice
¼ tsp. nutmeg
¼ cup coconut flour
¼ tsp. baking powder

Preheat oven to 400°F.
Line a 6-cup muffin pan with paper baking cups.

In a large bowl, mix the eggs, melted butter, pumpkin puree, sugar, cinnamon, allspice and nutmeg with a hand mixer until well combined.

Sift in coconut flour and baking powder and continue to mix until there are no lumps.

Spoon the batter into prepared muffin cups.
Bake 18 to 20 minutes or until wooden toothpick inserted in center comes out clean.

Makes 6 muffins

Pumpkin Muffins

Vegetables &

Side Dishes

Spinach Salad

SALAD
3 cups baby spinach, washed and dried
1 cup canned or cooked chickpeas, drained
½ red onion, thinly sliced

DRESSING
1 tbsp. balsamic vinegar
3 tbsp. extra virgin olive oil
Sea salt and pepper
¼ cup chopped walnuts (*optional*)

WHEAT FREE
DAIRY FREE
GLUTEN FREE
VEGETARIAN
VEGAN
EGG FREE
SOY FREE
NUT FREE

Toss spinach, chickpeas and onion together in a large bowl.

In a small bowl, whisk together vinegar and oil. Season to taste with salt and pepper. Pour dressing over salad and top with walnuts (*if desired*) and serve.

Makes 4 servings

Cucumber Salad

SALAD
1 large cucumber, seeded and sliced
2 large tomatoes, sliced
⅓ cup chopped red onion

DRESSING
2 tbsp. extra virgin olive oil
3 tbsp. balsamic vinegar
1 tsp. raw honey
Sea salt and pepper.
1 to 2 tbsp. chopped mint or parsley leaves

WHEAT FREE
DAIRY FREE
GLUTEN FREE
VEGETARIAN
EGG FREE
SOY FREE
NUT FREE

Toss cucumber, tomatoes and onion together in a large bowl.

In a small bowl, whisk together oil, vinegar and honey. Season to taste with salt and pepper. Pour dressing over salad. Add chopped mint or parsley and serve.

Makes 4 servings

Bean Sprout Salad

Mung bean sprouts, also known as bean sprouts, are often used in Asian cuisine. They are packed with vitamins and minerals including calcium, magnesium, potassium, phosphorus and Vitamin A.

WHEAT FREE
DAIRY FREE
GLUTEN FREE
VEGETARIAN
EGG FREE
NUT FREE

SALAD
3 cups bean sprouts
2 cups thinly sliced vegetables of choice
(peppers, zucchini, carrots etc.)

DRESSING
1 tbsp. Bragg All Purpose Seasoning or wheat-free soy sauce
2 tbsp. apple cider vinegar
2 tsp. sesame oil
1 tbsp. flax oil
1 garlic clove, minced
½ tsp. raw honey

GARNISH
1 green onion, chopped
1 to 2 tbsp. sesame seeds

Blanch bean sprouts in a large pot of boiling water for 30 seconds. Drain and set aside.

In a large bowl, combine the dressing ingredients. Add mung beans and vegetables. Mix well.

Cover and refrigerate overnight.

To serve, garnish with green onion and sesame seeds.

Makes 4 to 6 servings

Stuffed Zucchini

This is a great way to use up leftover rice. The recipe isn't limited to zucchini; try it with peppers tomatoes and other vegetables. Pictured on page 64.

WHEAT FREE

DAIRY FREE

GLUTEN FREE

VEGETARIAN

VEGAN

EGG FREE

NUT FREE

Stuffed Zucchini
2 whole zucchini (*about 8 inches long*)
1 cup cooked brown rice
¼ cup salsa
½ cup tomato sauce, divided

Preheat oven to 350°F.

Cut each zucchini in half. Scoop out and discard center, leaving about ¼ inch around the sides. Be careful not to puncture skin.

In a small bowl, mix together cooked rice, salsa and ¼ cup tomato sauce. Spoon rice mixture into the zucchini.

Place zucchini in a small baking dish. Cover and bake 25 minutes or until zucchini is tender.

Serve topped with reserved tomato sauce.

Makes 4 servings

Easy Brown Rice
3 cups water or vegetable broth
½ cup wild rice
1 cup brown rice
2 tsp. Bragg All Purpose Seasoning or wheat-free soy sauce

In a rice cooker, combine all ingredients. Cook according to manufacturers directions, approximately 35 to 40 minutes.

Makes 4 to 6 servings

Baked Falafel

These falafels are baked instead of deep fried.

WHEAT FREE
DAIRY FREE
GLUTEN FREE
VEGETARIAN
VEGAN
EGG FREE
SOY FREE
NUT FREE

1 (19 oz.) can chickpeas, drained and rinsed
  or 2 cups of cooked chickpeas
1 shallot or small onion, chopped
1 clove garlic, chopped
1 tsp. ground cumin
1 tsp. ground coriander
¼ tsp. sea salt
⅓ cup chopped fresh parsley
2 tbsp. extra virgin olive oil, divided

Preheat oven to 425°F.
Line a baking sheet with parchment paper.

Place chickpeas, onion, garlic, cumin, coriander, salt, parsley and
one tablespoon olive oil in the bowl of food processor.

Cover and process for several seconds until mixture is slightly coarse
but holds together when shaped into a ball.

Form chickpea mixture into golf-sized balls and place on prepared
baking sheet. Leave round or flatten slightly.

Brush falafel balls with remaining olive oil.

Bake 25 minutes or until golden brown and crispy. Turn once mid-
way through baking.

Serve with fresh homemade pita (page 55), cucumber, tomato,
lettuce, hummus, and tahini sauce (page 35).

Makes 12 falafel balls

Baked Falafels with Spelt Pita Bread (page 55)
and Tahini Sauce (page 35)

Rice Paper Rolls

WHEAT FREE

DAIRY FREE

GLUTEN FREE

VEGETARIAN

VEGAN

EGG FREE

Rolls
½ (400g) package vermicelli brown rice noodles
1 tsp. Bragg All Purpose Seasoning

Almond Dipping Sauce
2 tbsp. almond butter
1 tbsp. Bragg All Purpose Seasoning
2 tbsp. water

Wrappers
1 package rice paper wrappers
½ cup chopped cilantro, mint or parsley

Your choice of Filling (thinly sliced)
Peppers, cucumber, avocado, steamed asparagus, carrots
steamed Green beans, sprouts, omelet

In a large pot, bring 3 cups of boiling water along with 1 teaspoon
Bragg All Purpose Seasoning to a boil. Add noodles and cook
approximately three minutes or until softened. Drain and set aside.

Meanwhile, prepare dipping sauce. Whisk ingredients together in a
small bowl. Continue to whisk until the mixture resembles a smooth
paste. Set aside.

Assemble the rolls. In a large bowl of warm water, soak a rice paper
wrapper for 30 seconds or until soft. Remove wrapper to a paper
towel to absorb excess water.

About one-third from the bottom of the wrapper, lay one forkful of
rice noodles, a pinch of cilantro, and choice of filling. Fold the
bottom of the rice paper wrapper over the vegetables. Tuck in the
sides and roll into a cigar shape. Repeat with remaining rice paper
wrappers.

Serve with almond dipping sauce.

Makes 4 to 6 servings

Vermicelli brown rice noodles

Rice paper wrappers

Rice Paper Rolls

Hummus

WHEAT FREE

DAIRY FREE

GLUTEN FREE

VEGETARIAN

VEGAN

EGG FREE

SOY FREE

NUT FREE

1 (19 oz.) can organic chick peas, drained
or 2 cups cooked chickpeas
¼ cup water or more
1 to 2 cloves garlic, crushed
Pinch of sea salt
¼ cup tahini (*sesame seed paste*)
Juice of 1 lemon
1 to 2 tbsp. extra virgin olive oil
1 teaspoon sesame seeds

Place chickpeas in the bowl of a food processor
along with water, garlic, salt, tahini and lemon juice. Cover and
process several seconds until smooth. Slowly add in olive oil and, if
needed, additional water. Process again until mixture has a rich and
creamy consistency.

Pour into a serving dish and garnish with sesame seeds.
Serve with fresh vegetables and spelt pita (page 55)

Makes 2 cups

Tahini Sauce

WHEAT FREE

DAIRY FREE

GLUTEN FREE

VEGETARIAN

VEGAN

EGG FREE

SOY FREE

NUT FREE

½ cup tahini (*sesame seed paste*)
1 clove garlic, crushed (*or more to taste*)
½ tsp. sea salt
2 tbsp. olive oil
¼ cup lemon juice
2 to 3 tbsp. warm water

In a blender combine tahini, garlic, salt, olive oil
and lemon juice. Process until smooth.

Slowly add water, 1 tablespoon at a time, until sauce
reaches desired consistency.

Serve with falafels (page 31).

Makes ¾ cup

Garlic Rapini

1 bunch rapini, washed
1 to 2 tbsp. extra virgin olive oil
2 cloves garlic, minced

Trim rapini by removing the woody ends.

Place rapini in top part of double boiler. Place over gently boiling water; upper pan should not touch water. Steam rapini for about 6 minutes, or until tender. Set aside.

In a large skillet, heat oil over medium heat. Add garlic. Cook until fragrant.

Add rapini to skillet and heat through.

Makes 4 to 6 servings

WHEAT FREE
DAIRY FREE
GLUTEN FREE
VEGETARIAN
VEGAN
EGG FREE
SOY FREE
NUT FREE

Miso Coleslaw

Miso comes in many varieties, all with different flavours, depending on the base ingredient used to make it. The one I use in this recipe is the sweeter white or yellow type of miso.

WHEAT FREE

DAIRY FREE

GLUTEN FREE

VEGETARIAN

EGG FREE

NUT FREE

COLESLAW
2 cups green cabbage, thinly sliced (*about 2 cups*)
2 cups red cabbage, thinly sliced (*about 2 cups*)
3 carrots, thinly sliced
2 green onions, sliced

DRESSING
1 tbsp. white or yellow Miso paste
2 tsp Dijon mustard
1 tbsp. raw honey
3 tbsp. apple cider vinegar
4 tbsp. flax oil
1 tsp. toasted sesame oil

Toss cabbage, carrots and green onion together in a large bowl.

In a small bowl, prepare dressing by whisking ingredients together.

Pour dressing over cabbage. Toss to coat all ingredients.

Cover and refrigerate overnight.

Makes 4 to 6 servings

Miso Coleslaw

Soups

Cocoa Bean Soup

Cocoa Bean Soup

Cocoa powder adds a unique flavour to this wonderful soup.

2 tbsp. extra virgin olive oil
1 shallot or small onion, chopped
1 clove garlic, minced
½ cup chopped carrots
½ cup chopped celery
1 zucchini, chopped
½ cup salsa
½ tsp. cumin
½ tsp. cinnamon
½ tbsp. cocoa powder
1 cup vegetable broth
1 (14 oz.) can organic kidney beans, reserve liquid*

WHEAT FREE
DAIRY FREE
GLUTEN FREE
VEGETARIAN
VEGAN
EGG FREE
SOY FREE
NUT FREE

Heat oil in a heavy pot over medium heat. Add onion and garlic. Cook and stir until slightly browned.

Add carrots, celery, zucchini, salsa, cumin, cinnamon and cocoa powder. Cook 2 to 3 minutes until spices are fragrant.

Add broth, beans and reserved liquid.
*Note: If using non-organic beans, discard liquid and replace with one cup of vegetable broth.

Cover and bring soup to a boil. Reduce heat and simmer 20 minutes.

Remove from heat and let stand 10 minutes before serving.

Makes 4 servings

Lentil Soup

Rice Paper Rolls
(page 33)

Lentil Soup

A quick and easy one-pot meal.

1 sweet potato, peeled and cubed
1 shallot or small onion, chopped
5 cups vegetable broth
1 cup red lentils
1 cup chopped celery
1 cup chopped carrot
1 bay leaf

WHEAT FREE
DAIRY FREE
GLUTEN FREE
VEGETARIAN
VEGAN
EGG FREE
SOY FREE
NUT FREE

Combine all ingredients is a large pot. Bring to a boil.

Reduce heat and simmer 35 to 40 minutes.

Remove bay leaf.

Serve soup as is, or use a blender to process into a purée.

Makes 4 servings

Chunky Barley Soup

WHEAT FREE

DAIRY FREE

VEGETARIAN

VEGAN

EGG FREE

SOY FREE

NUT FREE

Barley is an excellent source of soluble fibre, which can help in lowering blood cholesterol levels.

Pot barley is not technically considered to be a whole grain, but is more nutrient dense than pearl barley.

1 tbsp. extra virgin olive oil
¼ cup chopped onion
1 clove garlic, crushed
1 (14 oz.) can diced tomatoes
1 cup chopped carrots
1 cup chopped celery
1 bay leaf
6 cups vegetable broth
⅓ cup pot barley, rinsed
1 small sweet potato, peeled and cubed
1 (15 oz.) can organic kidney beans, drained and rinsed

Heat oil in a large pot over medium heat. Add onion and garlic. Cook and stir until slightly browned.

Add tomatoes, carrots, celery, bay leaf, vegetable broth and barley. Bring to a boil then reduce heat and simmer 30 minutes.

Add sweet potato and kidney beans. Cover and cook an additional 30 minutes.

Remove bay leaf and serve.

Makes 4 servings

Chunky Barley Soup

Salmon Fingers
(page 68)

Miso Soup

Miso Soup

Miso is available in light and dark varieties. The light miso is sweeter whereas the darker miso will have a stronger flavour.

This recipe was prepared using dark, unfermented miso paste.

WHEAT FREE

DAIRY FREE

GLUTEN FREE

VEGETARIAN

VEGAN

EGG FREE

NUT FREE

Soup
4 cups water
1 cup thinly sliced vegetables (*carrots, watercress, zucchini, etc.*)
½ package enoki mushrooms
1½ tbsp. miso paste
1 tbsp. dried wakame flakes
1 green onion, thinly sliced

Bring 4 cups water to a boil in a large pot. Add sliced vegetables and mushrooms. Reduce heat and simmer 3 to 5 minutes.

Meanwhile, place miso paste in a small bowl. Stir in 1 to 2 tablespoons hot water to turn paste into a liquid. Set aside.

Remove soup from heat and stir in miso and wakame flakes.

Cover and let rest 5 minutes before serving.

Serve garnished with green onion.

Makes 4 servings

Roasted Butternut Squash Soup
with toasted pecans

Roasted Butternut Squash Soup

Other varieties of winter squash (such as acorn or hubbard) will also work well in this recipe.

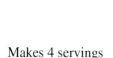

WHEAT FREE

DAIRY FREE

GLUTEN FREE

VEGETARIAN

VEGAN

EGG FREE

SOY FREE

¼ cup whole pecans
2 lbs. butternut squash or 2 cups cooked squash
1 tbsp. extra virgin olive oil
1 small onion, diced
1 clove garlic, minced
1 cup chopped carrots
1 cup chopped celery
1 small sweet potato, peeled and cubed
½ cup red lentils
6 cups vegetable broth
1 bay leaf

Preheat oven to 400°F.
Place pecans in a small baking dish and bake 3 to 5 minutes or until toasted. Remove from oven and cool before chopping. Set aside.

Rinse the squash under water to remove any dirt. Cut in half lengthwise and scoop out any seeds. Place cut squash facedown on parchment-lined baking sheet and bake 30 to 40 minutes, until a fork can easily pierce the skin. Remove from oven and cool. Once cool, scoop flesh into a bowl and set aside.

In a large pot, heat oil over medium heat. Add onion and garlic and cook until browned. Add carrots, celery, sweet potato, lentils, vegetable broth and bay leaf.

Cover and simmer 30 minutes. Remove bay leaf.
Cool slightly. Purée in a food processor or blender.

Serve garnished with toasted pecans.

 NUT FREE • Omit pecans

Makes 4 servings

Spinach Salad
(page 28)

Grains & Legumes

Pasta & Vegetable Sauté

Pasta & Vegetable Sauté

For a complete meal, add a protein source such as legumes, chicken or fish.

½ lb. brown rice pasta
4 tbsp. extra virgin olive oil
1 clove garlic, crushed
1 portobello mushroom, sliced
1 tsp. dried parsley
½ tsp. dried oregano
1 to 2 cups thinly sliced vegetables
(*zucchini, peppers, carrots, onion, etc.*)
Sea salt and pepper

WHEAT FREE
DAIRY FREE
GLUTEN FREE
VEGETARIAN
VEGAN
EGG FREE
SOY FREE
NUT FREE

In a large pot of salted boiling water, cook pasta according to package directions.

Meanwhile, heat oil in a non-stick pan over medium heat. Lightly sauté garlic until fragrant and lightly browned.

Add mushrooms, spices and sliced vegetables. Cook 3 to 5 minutes until vegetables are tender-crisp.

Drain pasta and transfer to a large bowl. Top with mushroom and vegetable mixture.

Season to taste with salt and pepper and serve.

Makes 2 to 4 servings

Quinoa Pilaf

Look for both red and white quinoa in your local health food store. This recipe was prepared using a combination of both.

1 cup quinoa
1 tbsp. extra virgin olive oil
1 garlic clove, minced
1 medium onion, diced
2 celery stalks, diced
2 carrots, diced
2 cups vegetable broth

WHEAT FREE
DAIRY FREE
GLUTEN FREE
VEGETARIAN
VEGAN
EGG FREE
SOY FREE
NUT FREE

Soak quinoa in water for at least 5 minutes. This will remove the bitter-tasting coating. Drain and rinse again.

In a medium-sized pot, heat oil over medium heat and sauté garlic until lightly browned. Add onion, celery and carrots and sauté for 3 minutes.

Add drained quinoa and broth.

Bring to a boil, then reduce heat and simmer 15 minutes.

Remove from heat and let stand, covered, for 5 minutes.

Fluff with a fork and serve.

Makes 4 servings

Risotto

Crimini mushrooms are also known as baby bellas, or portabellini mushrooms.

¼ cup chopped onion
1 cup sliced, crimini mushrooms
1 tbsp. extra virgin olive oil
1 cup long grain brown rice
1 cup peas, fresh or frozen
5 cups vegetable broth

WHEAT FREE
DAIRY FREE
GLUTEN FREE
VEGETARIAN
VEGAN
EGG FREE
SOY FREE
NUT FREE

In a heavy saucepan over medium heat, sauté onions and mushrooms in oil until vegetables begin to soften. (*If vegetables become too dry add ⅛ cup broth to help with the cooking process.*)

Add brown rice and toast slightly before adding 1 cup of broth.

Bring to a boil, then reduce heat and simmer. Add broth, one ladleful at a time. Cover and simmer rice between ladlefuls, allowing each ladleful to be absorbed before adding the next. (*If you run out of broth before the rice is cooked, add some boiling water.*)

Add fresh or frozen peas with last ladleful of broth.

Makes 4 servings

Brown Rice Sushi Rolls

WHEAT FREE

DAIRY FREE

GLUTEN FREE

VEGETARIAN

VEGAN

EGG FREE

NUT FREE

4 Nori Sheets
2 cups cooked, brown sushi rice (*page 54*)
½ cucumber, seeded and cut into matchsticks
½ avocado, peeled and thinly sliced
1 red pepper, seeded and cut into matchsticks
1 carrot, peeled and cut into matchsticks

To assemble rolls place 1 nori sheet, shiny side
down, on a bamboo rolling mat. (*I cover my mat with parchment
paper to help with cleanup*)

With water-moistened hands or the back of a spoon, spread ½ cup of
sushi rice evenly over the nori sheet, leaving about an inch space at
the top.

Arrange the cucumber, avocado, pepper and carrot in a narrow row
across the bottom third of the sushi rice.

Carefully begin rolling your roll from the bottom, using your
bamboo mat as a guide. The first roll should completely cover the
vegetables. (*Make sure you don't roll the bamboo mat into the roll
you're making.*) Continue to roll and tighten as you go, the same way
you would a rug to minimize excess space.

Let sushi roll stand a few minutes before cutting into 6 or 8 equal
pieces. Repeat with remaining nori sheets.

Serve with Bragg All Purpose Seasoning or wheat-free soy sauce.

Makes 4 rolls or 24 to 32 sushi rounds

Brown Sushi Rice

⅔ cup short-grain brown rice
2 cups water
2 tbsp. Bragg All Purpose Seasoning, divided
2 tbsp. rice vinegar

In a rice cooker combine brown rice, water and 1 tablespoon Bragg All Purpose Seasoning. Cook 35 to 40 minutes. Once cooked remove from heat and let rice stand, covered, 10 minutes.

While rice is standing, stir together vinegar and remaining tablespoon of Bragg All Purpose Seasoning .

Sprinkle vinegar mixture over rice, tossing gently with a large spoon to combine. Keep warm until ready to use.

WHEAT FREE
DAIRY FREE
GLUTEN FREE
VEGETARIAN
VEGAN
EGG FREE
NUT FREE

Makes 4 cups

Brown Rice Sushi Rolls

Spelt Pita Bread

WHEAT FREE

DAIRY FREE

VEGETARIAN

EGG FREE

SOY FREE

NUT FREE

3 cups spelt flour
1½ tsp. sea salt
1 tbsp. raw honey
1 (8g) packet instant yeast
2 tbsp. extra virgin olive oil
1 cup water, room temperature

In a large bowl, mix together flour, salt, honey,
and yeast. Add oil and water and stir together to form a dough.
Using your hands, make sure to incorporate all the flour. Use
additional water or flour if needed.

Knead dough by pressing the palms of the hands into the dough and
rotating 90 degrees each time. Knead the dough until stretchy and
elastic, about 10 minutes.

Place dough in a lightly oiled bowl. Cover with damp towel and let
rise 90 minutes.

Once risen, punch down dough to release trapped gas and divide into
10 equal pieces. Roll each piece into a ball and place on floured
surface. Cover and let rest 20 minutes.

Place a baking sheet or baking stone in the oven and preheat oven to
400°F.

Roll out each ball of dough, using additional flour if needed to keep
dough from sticking. Flatten to ¼-inch thickness. Cover and let rest
for an additional 10 to 15 minutes.

Place pitas on hot baking pan or baking stone. Bake 5 minutes until
puffy. Remove pitas to a rack to cool. Store in an airtight container.

Makes 10 pitas

*Wheat-Free Bread Crumbs: break stale pitas into small pieces and place on
baking sheet. Bake in a preheated 325°F oven until lightly browned then cool
completely. Place pieces in a food processor or blender and process until you
have a bread crumb consistency. Store in a sealed container.*

Spelt Pita Bread

Moroccan Chicken

Chicken & Fish

Moroccan Chicken

1 tbsp. extra virgin olive oil
1 lb. skinless, boneless chicken breast, cubed
½ onion, chopped
2 cloves garlic, chopped
2 carrots, sliced
2 celery stalks, sliced
½ sweet potato, cubed
½ tsp. paprika
½ tsp. ground cumin
½ tsp. dried oregano
¼ tsp. turmeric
¼ tsp. cinnamon
1 cup chicken broth
1 cup chopped tomatoes
1 (14 oz.) can organic chickpeas, drained
Sea salt and pepper

WHEAT FREE

DAIRY FREE

GLUTEN FREE

EGG FREE

SOY FREE

NUT FREE

Heat oil in a large saucepan over medium heat. Brown chicken until almost cooked through. Remove chicken and set aside.

In the same pan, sauté the onion, garlic, carrots, celery and sweet potato for 3 to 4 minutes using some broth if necessary to keep vegetables from sticking to the pan.

Add spices, chicken broth and tomatoes. Bring to a boil, then reduce heat and simmer. Add chicken and chickpeas.

Cover and simmer 20 to 25 minutes, making sure chicken is cooked through. Season to taste with salt and pepper.

Makes 4 servings

Almond Chicken Stir-fry

WHEAT FREE

DAIRY FREE

GLUTEN FREE

EGG FREE

Stir-fry Sauce
3 tbsp. Bragg All Purpose Seasoning
1 tbsp. almond butter
1-inch piece fresh ginger, peeled and grated
or 1 tsp. ground ginger
1 tsp. honey
1 tsp. cornstarch or tapioca flour
1 tsp. sesame oil
⅓ cup water

Stir-fry
1 lb. boneless, skinless chicken breasts, thinly sliced
3 tsp. extra virgin olive oil, divided
1 cup sliced white mushrooms
2 carrots, sliced
2 cups broccoli flowerets
1 cup snow peas, strings removed
¼ cup chicken broth
1 cup mung bean sprouts
2 green onions, thinly sliced
1 tbsp. sesame seeds

Prepare the stir-fry sauce by combining all ingredients in a bowl. Set aside.

In a medium bowl, toss chicken with 2 tablespoons of stir-fry sauce. Marinate 30 minutes or overnight.

In a non-stick skillet, heat 2 teaspoons of olive oil over medium heat. Add chicken and sauté until cooked through. Transfer to a platter and set aside.

In same skillet, heat remaining oil. Add mushrooms, carrots, broccoli and snow peas. Cook for an additional five minutes or until vegetables are tender-crisp stirring frequently and adding broth as needed to keep skillet from drying out.

Continued on next page

Almond Chicken Stir-fry

Pour remaining stir-fry sauce over vegetables and simmer 1 minute or until thickened. Return chicken to pan and add bean sprouts. Heat through.

Serve over brown rice (page 30), garnished with green onion and sesame seeds.

Makes 4 servings

Bruschetta-topped Chicken

WHEAT FREE

DAIRY FREE

SOY FREE

NUT FREE

2 boneless, skinless chicken breasts
   or 4 chicken cutlets
6 ripe plum tomatoes, chopped
2 cloves garlic, minced
1 tbsp. extra virgin olive oil
¼ cup chopped fresh parsley or basil leaves
1 egg
1 to 2 cups wheat free bread crumbs
¼ tsp. sea salt
⅛ tsp. pepper

Preheat oven to 425°F.
Lightly oil a baking sheet.

If using whole chicken breasts, butterfly or slice each breast into 2
cutlets. Using a meat mallet, gently pound the meat down to
¼-inch thickness.

In a small bowl, combine tomatoes, garlic and olive oil. Add parsley
or basil. Mix well and set aside.

In a separate bowl, whisk the egg and set aside.

In a shallow dish, combine bread crumbs with salt and pepper.

Dip each cutlet into egg to coat, then transfer to breadcrumb mixture,
making sure to coat both sides. Arrange on prepared baking sheet.

Bake cutlets 10 minutes or until cooked through and crust is golden
brown. Remove from oven and top with tomato mixture. Return to
oven and bake an additional 5 minutes.

Makes 4 servings

Spinach Salad
(page 28)

Bruschetta-topped Chicken

Rosemary Chicken Kebabs

WHEAT FREE
DAIRY FREE
GLUTEN FREE
EGG FREE
SOY FREE
NUT FREE

Marinade
3 tbsp. extra virgin olive oil
1½ tbsp. lemon juice
½ tsp. paprika
1 green onion, finely chopped
2 garlic cloves, minced
¼ tsp. sea salt
1 tbsp. chopped fresh parsley or 1 tsp. dried

Chicken
1 lb. boneless, skinless chicken breasts, cubed
2 small zucchini
4 to 6 fresh rosemary sprigs

Prepare marinade by combining ingredients in a small bowl. Pour over cubed chicken. Marinate 30 minutes or overnight.

Slice the zucchini lengthwise into ¼-inch strips. In a pot of boiling water, blanch the zucchini strips for 45 seconds or until they are pliable (*if overcooked they will not skewer well*). Drain and allow to cool.

Preheat broiler.

Using a rosemary sprig as a skewer, weave strips of zucchini between pieces of chicken. Place kebab in ungreased baking pan. Repeat with remaining chicken and zucchini. Pour any remaining marinade over kebabs.

Grill under broiler for 5 minutes or until chicken is cooked through.

Makes 4 to 6 servings

Rosemary Chicken Kebabs

Stuffed Zucchini
(page 30)

Omega-3 Burgers

WHEAT FREE

DAIRY FREE

SOY FREE

A quick and easy meal that's high in Omega-3s.

1 (213g) can wild salmon, drained
2 cups fresh baby spinach, finely chopped
½ cup wheat-free bread crumbs
1 egg
1 cup walnuts, chopped (*or any nut or seed of choice*)
1 cup fresh or frozen peas
1 tsp. lemon juice
¼ tsp. sea salt
Pinch of pepper

Preheat oven to 375°F.
Line a baking sheet with parchment paper.

In a large bowl, mix salmon, spinach, bread crumbs, egg, nuts, fresh or frozen peas, lemon juice, salt and pepper until well combined.

Divide mixture into 4 parts. Shape each part into a patty, and place on prepared baking sheet.

Bake 20 to 25 minutes.

Makes 4 patties

Omega-3 Burgers

Spinach Salad
(page 28)

Chunky Barley
Soup
(Page 43)

Salmon Fingers

Salmon Fingers

This recipe can easily be made with cod, haddock, chicken or turkey.

WHEAT FREE

DAIRY FREE

SOY FREE

NUT FREE

1 lb. wild salmon fillets
1 egg
¼ tsp. sea salt
⅛ tsp. pepper
1 cup wheat-free bread crumbs
2 tbsp. sesame seeds

Preheat oven to 425°F.
Lightly grease a baking sheet.

Cut salmon fillets into 1-inch-wide fingers and set aside.

In a small bowl, whisk together egg, salt and pepper.

In a shallow dish or pie plate, combine the bread crumbs and sesame seeds.

Dip each salmon finger into egg mixture to coat, then transfer to bread crumb mixture, making sure to coat all sides.

Arrange salmon on prepared baking sheet and bake 20 minutes or until cooked through.

Makes 2 to 4 servings

Desserts

Triple Berry Parfait
with Whipped Topping (page 71)

Triple Berry Parfait

A deliciously light treat that's sure to please the whole family.

WHEAT FREE
DAIRY FREE
GLUTEN FREE
VEGETARIAN
SOY FREE

3 eggs
2 tbsp. coconut butter, melted
2 tbsp. almond milk
3 tbsp. honey
¼ tsp. salt
¼ tsp. vanilla extract
¼ cup coconut flour
¼ tsp. baking powder
1 whipped topping recipe (page 71)
Fresh berries

Preheat oven to 400°F.
Line a 6-cup muffin pan with paper baking cups.

With a hand mixer blend together eggs, coconut butter, milk, honey, salt and vanilla in a large bowl.

Sift in the coconut flour and baking powder. Continue mixing until there are no lumps. Spoon batter into muffin cups.

Bake 15 minutes or until wooden toothpick inserted in center comes out clean.

Transfer cakes to a wire rack and cool completely.
Once cooled, cut each cake into 2 layers.

To assemble parfaits
In a parfait glass, alternate layers of berries, whipped topping and cake.

 NUT FREE   •   Replace almond milk with rice milk

Makes 6 parfaits

Whipped Topping

A dairy-free topping that can be used for all your favourite desserts.

1 (400 ml) can coconut milk*, chilled
1 tbsp. agave syrup
1 tsp. vanilla extract

On your counter or tabletop, turn the chilled can of coconut milk upside down. Puncture holes in the bottom of the can and drain any liquid into a cup. Discard the liquid or reserve for other recipes that call for milk.

Once liquid has been drained, use a can opener to open both ends of the can so that you can easily scoop the solidified coconut milk into a large bowl.

Add agave syrup and vanilla extract.

Beat with a hand mixer until the solidified coconut milk is light and fluffy.

To keep whipped topping firm, refrigerate until ready to use.

Note: Low-fat coconut milk is not recommended for this recipe.

*Coconut milk can differ from one company to another. When choosing a coconut milk from the store, give the can a shake. For best results choose a can in which a minimal amount of liquid can be heard.

Black Forest Cocoa Bites

WHEAT FREE

DAIRY FREE

GLUTEN FREE

VEGETARIAN

VEGAN

EGG FREE

SOY FREE

10 medjool dates, pitted
¼ cup dried cherries
1½ cups walnuts
¼ cup cocoa powder
½ tsp. vanilla extract

Soak dates and cherries in hot water for 5 minutes or until softened. Drain and set aside.

Place walnuts in a food processor. Cover and process for several seconds until walnuts are finely ground.

Add dates, cherries, cocoa and vanilla. Cover and process until mixture comes together. The mixture should hold together when shaped into a ball.

Transfer mixture onto a large square of parchment paper. Flatten to 1-inch thickness. Use the sides of the parchment paper to shape the mixture.

Cut into bite-sized squares and serve.

Makes 16 squares

Black Forest Cocoa Bites

Pumpkin Pie

WHEAT FREE

DAIRY FREE

VEGETARIAN

SOY FREE

NUT FREE

1 wheat-free pie crust (page 75)
2 cups fresh or canned pumpkin puree
¼ cup unsweetened applesauce
1 egg
¼ cup agave syrup
½ tsp. cinnamon
½ tsp. allspice
½ tsp. nutmeg
1 tsp. vanilla extract
½ cup coconut milk
2 tsp. cornstarch

Preheat oven to 375°F.

Fit the pie crust dough into a 9-inch pie plate and trim edges.
Reserve any leftover dough to decorate top. Pre-bake for 8 to 10
minutes or until crust just begins to brown. Remove from oven and
cool.

In a large bowl, combine pumpkin puree, applesauce, egg, syrup,
cinnamon, allspice, nutmeg, vanilla, coconut milk and cornstarch
with hand mixer until smooth.

Pour the filling into the cooled pie crust. Decorate top with any
reserved dough.

Bake 1 hour or until filling has set. If crust begins to brown too
quickly cover edges with foil and continue to bake.

Cool and serve with whipped topping (page 71) or maple walnut ice
cream (page 76).

Pumpkin Tarts with pecan topping *(as shown on page 75)*

Roll out pie crust and cut out circles to fit tart pan or muffin cups.
Pre-bake pie dough as above. Cool slightly. Fill with pumpkin
filling and top with chopped pecans. Bake 25 minutes or until set.

Pumpkin Pie

Pie Crust

A light and flaky pie crust.

2 cups spelt flour
1 tsp. baking powder
½ tsp. salt
1 tsp. agave syrup
⅔ cup coconut butter
1 tsp. apple cider vinegar
2 to 3 tbsp. ice cold water

WHEAT FREE
DAIRY FREE
VEGETARIAN
VEGAN
EGG FREE
SOY FREE
NUT FREE

In a small bowl, combine flour, baking powder and salt. Empty mixture into the bowl of a food processor and add syrup and coconut butter. Cover and process until mixture forms clumps about the size of small peas.

Sprinkle in apple cider vinegar and 2 tablespoons of water. Process again until it forms a ball. (*If too dry, continue to add water until mixture forms a ball. If too wet, add additional flour.*)

Set aside to rest for 15 minutes.

Remove dough from food processor and place onto a sheet of parchment paper. Flour lightly and cover with an additional sheet of parchment paper. Flatten dough between the 2 sheets of parchment paper, with rolling pin, to desired thickness.

Makes 1 pie crust

Pumpkin Tart
(page 73)

Maple Walnut Ice Cream

Maple Walnut Ice Cream

A wonderful dairy-free ice cream.

1½ cups cashews
1½ cups almond milk
¾ cup pure maple syrup
1 tsp. vanilla extract
1 cup walnuts, chopped

WHEAT FREE
DAIRY FREE
GLUTEN FREE
VEGETARIAN
VEGAN
EGG FREE
SOY FREE

Prepare your ice cream maker according to manufacturer's directions.

Place cashews in a food processor. Cover and process several seconds until finely ground.

In a blender, add ground cashews, almond milk, maple syrup and vanilla. Cover and blend until smooth.

Refrigerate mixture 1 hour or overnight.

Pour mixture and chopped walnuts into ice cream maker. Process according to manufacturer's directions.

For soft serve ice cream, serve immediately.

Note: To prepare perfect scoops of ice cream line a 12-cup muffin pan with paper liners and fill with scoops of ice cream. Freeze for about 2 hours or until firm. For longer storage, transfer to an airtight container until you are ready to serve.

Makes 12 scoops of ice cream

Chocolate Cupcakes

A light and fluffy cake with a secret ingredient ... black beans!

WHEAT FREE
DAIRY FREE
GLUTEN FREE
VEGETARIAN
SOY FREE
NUT FREE

1 (14 oz.) can organic black beans
4 eggs
½ cup agave syrup
3 tbsp. dark cocoa powder
1 tsp. baking powder
½ tsp. baking soda
2 tbsp. safflower oil or coconut butter, melted
1 tsp. vanilla extract

Preheat oven to 350°F.
Line a 12-cup muffin pan with paper baking cups.

Drain and rinse black beans well.

In a blender, combine black beans, eggs, agave syrup, cocoa, baking powder, baking soda, oil and vanilla extract.

Cover and blend all ingredients until black beans have been fully puréed.

Pour the batter into prepared muffin cups.

Bake 20 to 25 minutes or until wooden toothpick inserted in center comes out clean.

Makes 12 cupcakes

Chocolate Cupcakes

Date Squares

WHEAT FREE

DAIRY FREE

VEGETARIAN

VEGAN

EGG FREE

SOY FREE

NUT FREE

Filling
1½ cups chopped dates
¾ cup apple juice
1 tsp. vanilla extract

Crust / Topping
1 cup spelt flour
½ cup rolled oats
⅛ cup agave syrup
¼ tsp. sea salt
⅓ cup coconut butter

Preheat oven to 350°F.
Line an 8-inch square baking pan with parchment paper.

In a small saucepan over low heat, cook dates in apple juice, stirring frequently until mixture forms a thick paste. Remove from heat and stir in vanilla.

In a large bowl, combine the flour, oats, agave syrup and salt. Add coconut butter and mix in with your hands or a fork until you have a crumb-like consistency.

Pour three-quarters of the crumb mixture into prepared baking pan, reserving the remaining mixture for the top. Pat the crust mixture down firmly in the pan.

Pre-bake the crust 15 to 20 minutes or until slightly browned. Remove from oven and cool slightly.

Spread filling mixture over baked crust and sprinkle remaining crumb mixture on top.

Return to oven and bake 30 to 35 minutes.

Makes 8 squares

Date Squares

Chocolate Pudding

Chocolate Pudding

This recipe is for my husband, who loves his pudding!

1½ cups almond milk, divided
⅓ cup agave syrup
¼ cup cocoa powder
1 tsp. vanilla extract
¼ tsp. sea salt
2½ tbsp. cornstarch or tapioca flour

WHEAT FREE
DAIRY FREE
GLUTEN FREE
VEGETARIAN
VEGAN
EGG FREE
SOY FREE

Combine 1 cup of almond milk with agave syrup in a small pot and simmer over medium heat.

Meanwhile, in a large mixing cup, combine the remaining milk, cocoa powder, vanilla, salt and cornstarch. Mix well, until cornstarch and cocoa are dissolved.

Slowly pour cocoa mixture into simmering milk. Whisk until mixture thickens (*approximately 2 to 3 minutes*).

Remove from heat and pour into 4 small serving dishes or 2 larger dishes.

Cover and refrigerate several hours until set.

 NUT FREE

• Replace almond milk with rice milk

Makes 2 to 4 servings

Gingerbread Cookies

WHEAT FREE

DAIRY FREE

VEGETARIAN

SOY FREE

NUT FREE

*This dough is perfect for creating all
your gingerbread creations.*

¾ cup coconut butter, softened
1 cup sucanat sugar
1 egg
¼ cup organic molasses
2½ cups spelt flour
2 tsp. baking powder
1 tsp. cinnamon
1 tsp. ground ginger
¼ tsp. sea salt

Preheat oven to 350°F.
Line several baking sheets with parchment paper.

In a large bowl, beat butter and sugar with hand mixer on low speed,
until creamy. Add egg and molasses. Mix until well combined.

Sift in flour, baking powder, cinnamon, ginger and sea salt.
Continue mixing until well combined. Add more flour if dough is too
sticky.

Cover and let rest 1 hour.

Separate the dough into halves. On a lightly floured surface, working
with a half at a time, roll out to ⅛-inch thickness. Cut out cookies
using your favourite cookie cutters. Transfer cookies onto prepared
baking sheet, placing about 1 inch apart. Reroll trimmings and
continue to cut out shapes.

Bake 8 to 10 minutes or until edges are lightly browned.

Transfer cookies to cooling racks and cool completely before
decorating.

Makes 24 small cookies

Gingerbread Cookies

Cream Puffs

Impress your guests with this tasty and elegant dessert.

WHEAT FREE

DAIRY FREE

GLUTEN FREE

VEGETARIAN

SOY FREE

NUT FREE

½ cup water
¼ cup coconut butter
Pinch of salt
1 tsp. agave syrup
½ cup brown rice flour
2 eggs
1 custard recipe (page 88)
2 oz. dark chocolate (*optional*)

Preheat oven 425°F.
Line a baking sheet with parchment paper.

In a saucepan, mix the coconut butter, salt and agave syrup with the water and bring to a boil. Remove from heat and immediately add all of the flour. Beat with a wooden spoon until the dough forms a ball and comes away from the sides of the pan.

Add 1 egg one at a time, fully incorporating each egg before adding the next.

Using a spoon, drop mounds of dough on prepared baking sheet, spacing mounds 1 to 2 inches apart.

Bake 20 to 25 minutes or until golden brown. Turn off oven and open door slightly. Leave puffs to sit in oven for an additional 7 to 10 minutes before removing from oven to cool completely.

Meanwhile, prepare the custard recipe, page 88.

To fill the puffs, cut off their tops and spoon in custard filling. Replace tops. If desired, melt chocolate and drizzle over puffs.

Makes 12 puffs

TIP: Best assembled just before serving.

Cream Puffs
with Custard filling (page 89)

Almond Treats

WHEAT FREE

DAIRY FREE

GLUTEN FREE

VEGETARIAN

SOY FREE

A simple and not-too-sweet almond treat.

2 egg whites, room temperature
Pinch of salt
1 tsp. almond extract
¼ cup sucanat sugar
2 cup almonds, finely ground
12 whole almonds

Preheat oven to 350°F.
Line a large baking sheet with parchment paper.

In a large bowl, whip egg whites and salt with a hand mixer until they become white and begin to stiffen. Add almond extract.

Add half the sugar at a time, whipping between additions. Continue to mix until the egg whites are very stiff. Use a rubber spatula to fold in ground almonds.

Fill a pastry bag with the almond mixture. Pipe mounds onto the parchment paper, spacing about 1 inch apart.

Top each cookie with a whole almond.

Bake 20 minutes or until firm to the touch and lightly browned along the edges.

Makes 12 cookies

Custard

A deliciously smooth, rich, and creamy filling that can be used for many desserts including Cream Puffs (page 85).

WHEAT FREE

DAIRY FREE

GLUTEN FREE

VEGETARIAN

SOY FREE

NUT FREE

¼ cup sucanat sugar
4 egg yolks*
3 tbsp. brown rice flour
Pinch of salt
1½ cups regular or low-fat coconut milk
1½ tsp. vanilla extract

In a small bowl, whisk together sugar and egg yolks until mixture is thick and pale.

Sift flour and salt into the eggs and beat well.

In a small saucepan, bring coconut milk to a boil, then reduce heat to a simmer.

Add ⅛ cup of hot milk into egg mixture and stir well.

Slowly whisk the egg mixture into the hot milk, stirring constantly. Bring custard to a simmer and cook 2 minutes or until thickened.

Remove from heat; cool slightly then stir in vanilla.

Refrigerate until completely cooled.

*Not sure what do you with your leftover egg whites?
Try making almond treats (page 87) or coconut treats (page 89).

Coconut Treats

A simple and easy coconut treat.

2 egg whites, room temperature
Pinch of sea salt
1 tsp. vanilla extract
¼ cup sucanat sugar
1 cup unsweetened shredded coconut
2 oz. dark chocolate

Preheat oven to 350°F.
Line small baking sheet with parchment paper.

In a large bowl, using a hand mixer, whip egg whites and salt until they become white and begin to stiffen. Stir in vanilla. Add half the sugar at a time, whipping between additions.

Continue to whip until the egg whites are stiff. Fold in coconut.

Drop a teaspoonful of the mixture onto prepared baking sheet leaving 1 to 2 inches between each cookie.

Bake 20 minutes or until firm to the touch and lightly browned along the edges. Remove from oven and cool completely.

Meanwhile, melt chocolate in a small heatproof bowl set over a pan of almost-simmering water, stirring once or twice, until smooth and melted.

Dip cookies into melted chocolate and place back on a the parchment-lined baking sheet.

Refrigerate for 30 minutes or until chocolate has set.

Makes 9 cookies

Coconut Treats

Recipe Index

Recipe Index

Recipe Index

Recipes Sorted by Category

Recipes Sorted by Category

Recipes Sorted by Category

About the Author

Rita Mustafa is the founder of Oasis Health
& Wellness and Oasis Kitchen. Rita is a
Holistic Nutritionist and a Registered
Traditional Chinese Acupuncturist.

Rita graduated from the Canadian School of
Natural Nutrition and the Ontario College
of Traditional Chinese Medicine.

Rita uses an individual approach to optimal wellness for each and
every client. "We are all unique" – no two people have the same
metabolism, biochemical make-up, health concerns, behavioural
issues or nutrition needs. Failing to address these issues when
designing a nutrition program can lead to poor results and
frustration. Rita's focus is on helping her clients to set realistic goals
and achieve lifelong health and wellness.

In her clinic, Rita counsels clients on a variety of health conditions
and issues including:

- Weight Management - Weight Loss
- PMS/Hormonal Imbalances
- Pre/Post-natal Nutrition
- Menopause Management
- Digestive Disorders
- Blood Sugar Imbalances (Diabetes, Hypoglycemia)
- Hypothyroidism
- Energy Problems
- Food Allergies and Sensitivities
- Osteoporosis

Rita lives in Markham, Ontario with her husband and two Shih Tzus.